Land of Liberty

New Hampshire

by Barbara Knox

Consultant:
Kenneth Relihan
Social Studies Consultant
New Hampshire Department
of Education
Concord, New Hampshire

Capstone press
Mankato, Minnesota

Capstone Press
151 Good Counsel Drive • P.O. Box 669 • Mankato, Minnesota 56002
http://www.capstone-press.com

Library of Congress Cataloging-in-Publication Data
Knox, Barbara.
    New Hampshire / by Barbara Knox.
        p. cm.—(Land of liberty)
    Includes bibliographical references and index.
    Contents: About New Hampshire—Land, climate, and wildlife—History
of New Hampshire—Government and politics—Economy and resources—People
and culture.
    ISBN 0-7368-2187-2 (hardcover)
    1. New Hampshire—Juvenile literature. [1. New Hampshire.] I. Title. II. Series.
F34.3.K58 2004
974.2—dc21   2002154996

Summary: An introduction to the geography, history, government, politics,
economy, resources, people, and culture of New Hampshire, including maps, charts,
and a recipe.

Editorial Credits
Angela Kaelberer and Tom Adamson, editors; Jennifer Schonborn, series designer;
    Molly Nei, book designer; Enoch Peterson, illustrator; Heather Atkinson and
    Jo Miller, photo researchers; Eric Kudalis, product planning editor

Photo Credits
Cover images: Marlow Village Pond, Dave MacKenzie; snow-covered trees in
New Hampshire, Index Stock Imagery/Frank Siteman

Ann & Rob Simpson, 57; Capstone Press/Gary Sundermeyer, 54; Corbis, 24–25, 27;
Corbis Sygma/Wyman Ira, 36; Corbis/Erik Freeland, 46; Digital Vision, 1; Getty
Images/Hulton Archive, 21, 58; Getty Images/Stock Montage/Archive Photos, 28, 30;
Index Stock Imagery/Steve Dunwell Photography Inc., 14; Index Stock Imagery/
Kindra Clineff, 16; Index Stock Imagery/Roger Leo, 38; Index Stock Imagery/Greig
Cranna, 42; Index Stock Imagery/Henryk T. Kaiser, 63; Kent & Donna Dannen, 56;
NASA, 52; New Hampshire Historical Society, 22; North Wind Picture Archives, 18;
One Mile Up Inc., 55 (both); Swenson Granite Company LLC, 44; Tom Till, 8;
Unicorn Stock Photos/Joseph L. Fontenot, 4; Unicorn Stock Photos/Andre Jenny,
12–13; Unicorn Stock Photos/Jean Higgins, 32; Unicorn Stock Photos/V. E. Horne,
50–51; U.S. Postal Service, 59; Visuals Unlimited/Warren Stone, 40–41

Artistic Effects
Corbis, Digital Vision, PhotoSpin, PhotoDisc Inc.

1 2 3 4 5 6 08 07 06 05 04 03

Table of Contents

Thousands of people climb Mount Monadnock every year.

Chapter 1

About New Hampshire

Every year, more than 100,000 people hike to the top of Mount Monadnock near Jaffrey, New Hampshire. Mount Monadnock is one of the most climbed mountains in the United States.

Mount Monadnock stands alone in the southwestern corner of New Hampshire. Since no other mountains are near, hikers have a clear view of the surrounding area. When hikers reach the top of the 3,165-foot (965-meter) mountain, they have a view of all six New England states. Besides New Hampshire, those states are Connecticut, Rhode Island, Massachusetts, Vermont, and Maine.

At least 12 trails lead to the top of Mount Monadnock. The trails cover more than 40 miles (64 kilometers). The oldest trail is called the White Arrow Trail. This trail dates back to 1706.

Granite State

New Hampshire is called the Granite State because of its rich deposits of granite. People cut blocks of the hard, gray stone out of the state's many quarries. Granite is often used in buildings and for gravestones.

New Hampshire is a northeastern state. The Canadian province of Quebec borders New Hampshire on the north. The Connecticut River separates New Hampshire from its western neighbor, Vermont. Massachusetts lies to the south. Maine and the Atlantic Ocean form the state's eastern border.

New Hampshire Cities

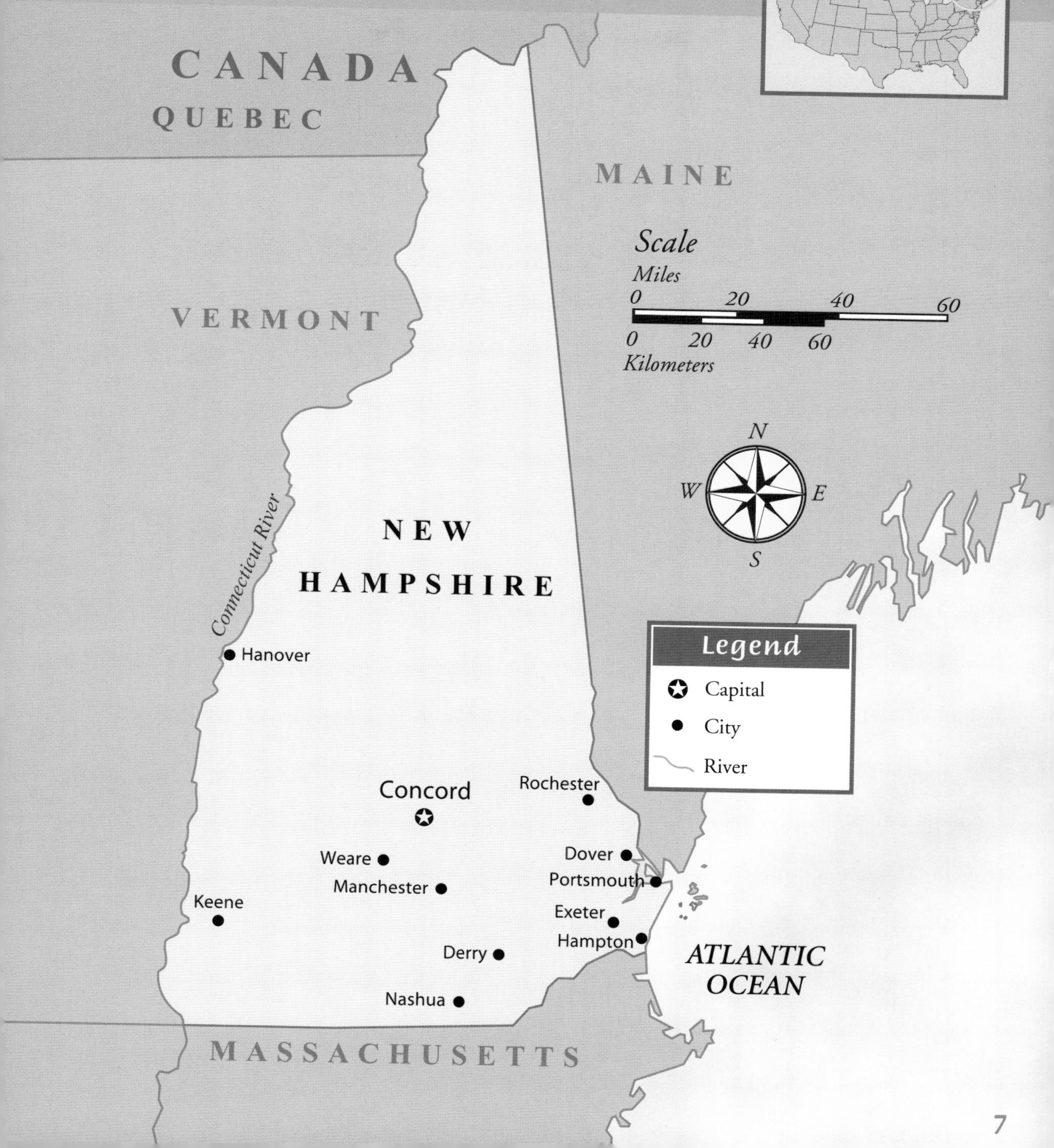

CANADA

QUEBEC

MAINE

VERMONT

Scale

Miles

| 0 | 20 | 40 | 60 |

| 0 | 20 | 40 | 60 |

Kilometers

Connecticut River

NEW
HAMPSHIRE

N

W E

S

Hanover

Legend

⭐ Capital

● City

〰 River

Concord
⭐

Rochester ●

Weare ●

Manchester ●

Dover ●

Portsmouth ●

Keene ●

Exeter ●

Hampton ●

Derry ●

ATLANTIC
OCEAN

Nashua ●

MASSACHUSETTS

The colorful fall leaves in the White Mountains make New Hampshire popular with tourists.

Chapter 2

Land, Climate, and Wildlife

Mountains, farmland, seashore, and lakes are all part of New Hampshire's geography. Thousands of years ago, glaciers carved the state's landscape. These large sheets of ice created mountains and lakes as they moved slowly across the land.

Today, New Hampshire can be divided into three main regions. These areas are the White Mountains, the Coastal Lowlands, and the Eastern New England Upland.

White Mountains

The White Mountains stretch from central New Hampshire into western Maine. The tops of the White Mountains have

Did you know...?
What may be the
northeastern United States'
oldest tree grows near
Northwood, New Hampshire.
Scientists believe this
blackgum tree is at least
700 years old.

few trees. Granite shows through the ground in many spots. From a distance, the mountains appear white.

Three ranges are part of the White Mountains. These are the Presidential Range, the Franconia Range, and the Sandwich Range.

The 86 mountains in the Presidential Range are the highest peaks in New England. Mount Washington is the highest of these peaks. This mountain is 6,288 feet (1,917 meters) high.

Another famous peak is in the Franconia Range. On the side of Cannon Mountain is a cliff that once looked like the face of an old man. People called it the Old Man of the Mountain. In 2003, the face crumbled. Years of wind, rain, and ice caused the granite ledges to collapse.

White Mountain National Forest covers much of the region. The forest covers 780,000 acres (315,666 hectares). About 94 percent of the forest is in New Hampshire. The rest of the forest stretches into Maine. Red maples and sugar maples are the most common trees in the forest.

Part of the Appalachian National Scenic Trail cuts through the forest. This hiking trail stretches 2,168 miles (3,489 kilometers) from Georgia to Maine. About 170 miles (274 kilometers) of the trail is in New Hampshire.

New Hampshire's Land Features

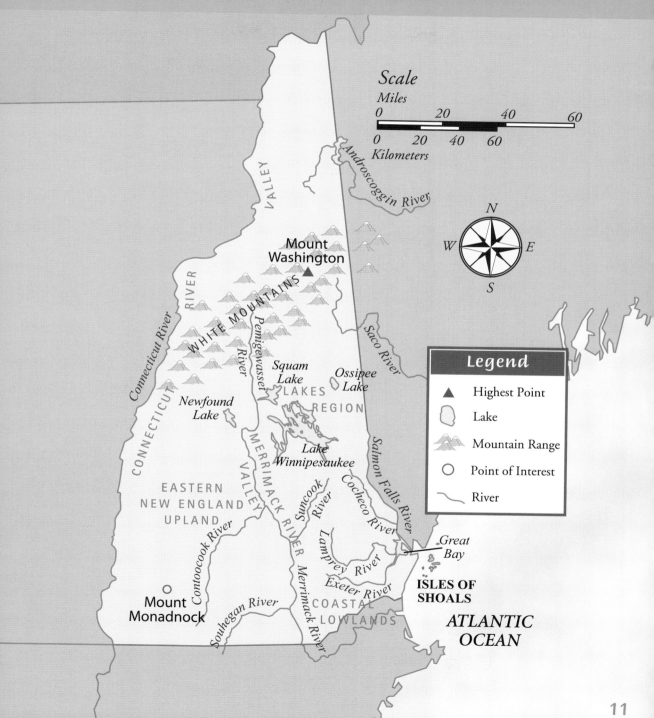

Scale

Miles

0   20   40   60

0   20   40   60

Kilometers

N
W   E
S

Androscoggin River

VALLEY

Mount Washington

WHITE MOUNTAINS

CONNECTICUT RIVER

Pemigewasset River

Saco River

Squam Lake

Ossipee Lake

LAKES REGION

Newfound Lake

MERRIMACK VALLEY

Lake Winnipesaukee

Salmon Falls River

Suncook River

Cocheco River

EASTERN NEW ENGLAND UPLAND

Contoocook River

Lamprey River

MERRIMACK RIVER

Great Bay

Mount Monadnock

Exeter River

ISLES OF SHOALS

Souhegan River

COASTAL LOWLANDS

ATLANTIC OCEAN

Legend

▲   Highest Point

⬭   Lake

⛰   Mountain Range

○   Point of Interest

〜   River

Crawford Notch State Park is also part of the White Mountains. In 1771, Timothy Nash found an opening in the mountains near Lancaster. This opening, or notch, allowed people to travel through the White Mountains to the Upper Connecticut River Valley. In the early 1800s, Abel Crawford built an inn near the notch. People started calling the opening Crawford Notch.

Coastal Lowlands

New Hampshire has only 13 miles (21 kilometers) of coastline along the Atlantic Ocean. Great Bay sits inland near

the town of Newmarket. Ocean tides flow into Great Bay twice each day. The ocean water mixes with fresh river water. The Squamscott, Exeter, Lamprey, and Winnicut Rivers drain into the bay.

Salt marshes near Great Bay provide homes for birds and wildlife, fish and shellfish, and many types of plants. The ocean tides and fresh river water feed the shallow marshes.

The Isles of Shoals lie about 9 miles (14 kilometers) off New Hampshire's coast. Four of these nine small islands are part of New Hampshire. The other five are part of Maine.

Portsmouth is one of New Hampshire's Atlantic coast cities.

Eastern New England Upland

The Eastern New England Upland is south of the White Mountains. The region covers southern New Hampshire.

Three smaller regions form the Eastern New England Upland. These regions are the Lakes Region, the Merrimack River Valley, and the Connecticut River Valley.

Lake Winnipesaukee is New Hampshire's largest lake.

The Lakes Region is in the foothills of the White Mountains. More than 250 lakes and ponds are found in this area. These lakes include the state's largest lake, Lake Winnipesaukee. This lake covers 71 square miles (184 square kilometers). Lake Winnisquam, Squam Lake, and Newfound Lake are other large lakes in the region.

The Merrimack River Valley lies in the middle of southern New Hampshire. The 110-mile (177-kilometer) Merrimack River carved the valley. Smaller rivers also flow through the valley. The Suncook, the Souhegan, and the Contoocook Rivers empty into the Merrimack River.

The Connecticut River forms the state's western border with Vermont. It is the state's longest river. About 211 miles (340 kilometers) of the river flow through New Hampshire.

Climate

New Hampshire summers are usually cool. The state's average summer temperature is 65 degrees Fahrenheit (18 degrees Celsius).

Mother of Rivers

New Hampshire has been called the Mother of Rivers. Some of New England's longest rivers begin in New Hampshire. The Connecticut River (right) begins in the north. The Pemigewasset River begins in Profile Lake in the Franconia Mountains. It joins the Winnipesaukee at Franklin to form the Merrimack River. At Dover, the Cocheco and Salmon Falls Rivers join to form the Piscataqua River. Two of Maine's longest rivers, the Androscoggin and the Saco, begin in northern New Hampshire.

New Hampshire winters are cold. Snow covers most of the state. The average winter temperature is 20 degrees Fahrenheit (minus 7 degrees Celsius).

Snow and rainfall vary in New Hampshire. The state receives an average of 42 inches (107 centimeters) of precipitation each year. The White Mountains receive between 52 and 96 inches (132 and 244 centimeters) of precipitation each year. Snow makes up much of this precipitation.

The weather station on Mount Washington has recorded some of the worst weather in the country. Winter winds of more than 70 miles (113 kilometers) per hour are common. In April 1934, weather instruments recorded winds of 231 miles (372 kilometers) per hour. In winter, temperatures can fall to minus 50 degrees Fahrenheit (minus 46 degrees Celsius). The top of the mountain receives an average of 21 feet (6.4 meters) of snow each year.

Wildlife

Native New Hampshire mammals include white-tailed deer, muskrats, beavers, porcupines, and snowshoe hares. Humpback whales, dolphins, and harbor seals swim near the coast.

The Atlantic coastal waters are filled with flounder, bluefish, Atlantic cod, and other saltwater fish. Mussels, clams, and other shellfish also live along the coast.

Many varieties of fish swim in the state's freshwater lakes and rivers. Large numbers of lake trout and brook trout make New Hampshire a favorite fishing spot.

New Hampshire's beaches, mountains, and forests provide homes for many types of birds. Cormorants, sandpipers, and gulls live along the coast. Inland, bird-watchers can spot mockingbirds, hawks, and finches.

Native people built houses called wigwams in what is now New Hampshire.

Chapter 3

History of New Hampshire

Native people lived near the New Hampshire coast at least 5,000 years before European explorers arrived. The native people were skillful hunters and fishers. They used dugout canoes to catch large deep-sea fish. But there is no detailed record of the daily lives of those early tribes.

By the early 1600s, two main groups of native people lived in what is now New Hampshire. The largest group was the Pennacook Confederacy. This group included the Pennacook, Nashua, Souhegan, Amoskeag, and Winnipesaukee. These tribes lived in what is now central and southern New Hampshire.

The other main group, the Abenaki Confederacy, lived in the eastern part of the state. This group included the Pequawket and the Ossipee.

European Settlement

Europeans came to what is now New Hampshire in the 1600s. In 1603, English Captain Martin Pring sailed along the coast and up the Piscataqua River. Two years later, Samuel de Champlain mapped the New England coastline for France. In 1614, Captain John Smith mapped the coastline for England.

The Council for New England was an English company established in New England during the early 1600s. The Council granted pieces of land to people who wanted to start businesses in North America. In 1622, the Council gave the first land grant in present-day New Hampshire. Englishmen Captain John Mason and Sir Ferdinando Gorges received this grant. In 1623, David Thomson and Edward Hilton received grants. Thomson built a settlement on the Piscataqua River near present-day Portsmouth. Hilton's group settled 8 miles (13 kilometers) upriver in what is now Dover.

Gorges and Mason divided their land grant in 1629. Gorges' part became Maine. Mason called his land New Hampshire after the county in England that had been his home. Settlers built the town of Exeter in 1638, followed by Hampton in 1639.

John Smith was one of the first European explorers to visit New England.

John Mason and Ferdinando Gorges divided their land grant in 1629. Mason named his part of the land New Hampshire.

The first four settlements of New Hampshire came under Massachusetts' rule in 1641. New Hampshire remained a part of Massachusetts until 1679, when King Charles II separated them. New Hampshire then became a royal province.

Land Disputes

New Hampshire grew slowly during the early years of the colony. After John Mason's death in 1635, his descendants claimed the right to his land in New Hampshire. The people who had settled the land refused to leave. The constant fighting over the land kept new settlers from moving to New Hampshire. In 1746, the disagreement was settled when 12 men from Portsmouth paid the Mason family members for the land.

Disagreements over land continued. In the mid-1700s, New York and New Hampshire fought over an area west of the Connecticut River called the New Hampshire Grants. In 1765, King George II decided New York would own the land. That land later became the state of Vermont. The king set the Connecticut River as New Hampshire's western border.

Revolution and Independence

In 1765, Great Britain passed the Stamp Act. This law taxed printed materials. The Stamp Act was followed by the Townshend Acts, which taxed tea and glass. The colonists protested the taxes. In 1770, Great Britain removed all taxes except the tea tax. This decision angered the colonists. Many wanted independence from Great Britain.

By the 1770s, the independence movement was in full force in New Hampshire. In 1774, British Governor John Wentworth II tried to break up a meeting of the New Hampshire Assembly. The assembly members moved their meeting to Exeter. They formed a provincial congress to govern the colony. They elected Josiah Bartlett and John Pickering to represent New Hampshire at the First

Continental Congress in Philadelphia. Groups of soldiers called militias began training throughout the colony.

On January 5, 1776, New Hampshire adopted its first constitution. Seven months later, representatives of all 13 colonies signed the Declaration of Independence. New Hampshire's constitution remained in force until 1784.

New Hampshire was the only colony that the British did not invade during the Revolutionary War (1775–1783). But New Hampshire soldiers fought hard for the colonies.

New Hampshire troops helped fight the British in the Battle of Bunker Hill near Boston.

"We have the full conviction that the time will come when the whole nation will give honors of the Battle of Bunker Hill largely to the common soldiers of New Hampshire who, more than any other men, fought it."

—Historian Increase Tarbox of Boston, Massachusetts

In 1775, more than 1,000 New Hampshire troops fought in the Battle of Bunker Hill near Boston. Shipyard workers in Portsmouth built ships for the war. In October 1781, the British surrendered to the Americans. In 1783, the Treaty of Paris ended the war.

On June 21, 1788, New Hampshire approved the U.S. Constitution and became the ninth state. Exeter was the state's first capital.

Beginning of Industry

By 1800, more than 183,000 people lived in New Hampshire. As its population grew, most of the state's business activity shifted from the coast to the Merrimack River Valley. The cities of Nashua and Manchester grew around the textile mills on the Merrimack River. A shoe factory opened in Weare in 1823.

In 1809, New Hampshire's first cotton mill was built on Amoskeag Falls near Manchester. By 1850, the Amoskeag

Children were among the workers at the Amoskeag Manufacturing Company.

Manufacturing Company was one of the largest textile mills in the world. At first, children operated the equipment in the textile mills. Later, the mills brought in adult workers from Quebec, Canada.

In the 1800s, tourism became an important industry in New Hampshire. Artists and writers came to see the state's

Franklin Pierce

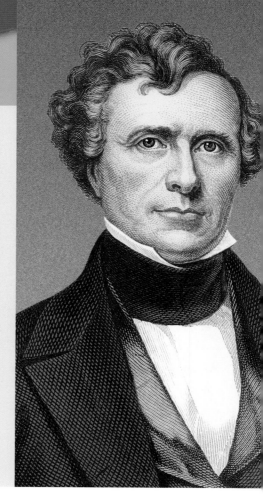

Franklin Pierce was born in Hillsboro on November 23, 1804. In 1829, Pierce was elected to the New Hampshire legislature. He served until 1833. Pierce went on to serve as a U.S. representative and U.S. senator from New Hampshire. In 1853, he became the 14th president.

Pierce supported the Kansas-Nebraska Act of 1854. This law allowed people in those states to decide if they wanted slavery to be legal. This law led to bloodshed in Kansas and set the stage for the Civil War. The Democratic Party refused to support Pierce for reelection. James Buchanan won the presidency in 1856. Pierce died October 8, 1869.

natural beauty. People built large hotels along the seashore and in the White Mountains.

In 1838, the state's first railroad connected Nashua with Lowell, Massachusetts. Railroads allowed New Hampshire farmers and factories to ship their products to large cities in nearby states. The railroads also brought visitors to the state.

By the 1850s, the country was divided over the issue of slavery. In 1860 and 1861, 11 Southern states left the Union and formed the Confederate States of America. During the Civil War (1861–1865), about 39,000 New Hampshire men fought for the Union. The state's huge textile mills provided material for blankets and uniforms for Union soldiers. Other factories made rifles and train locomotives for the war.

Hard Times

New Hampshire's textile industry began to fail in the 1920s. Many mills moved to the southern United States, where workers were willing to work for less money. As rayon and other new fabrics became popular, demand for cotton cloth decreased. The Great Depression (1929–1939) hurt the state's textile industry even more.

In 1941, the United States entered World War II (1939–1945). The war helped New Hampshire's manufacturing businesses. The Portsmouth Naval Shipyard built battleships and submarines. The state's factories made uniforms, boots, and blankets for U.S. soldiers.

Daniel Webster

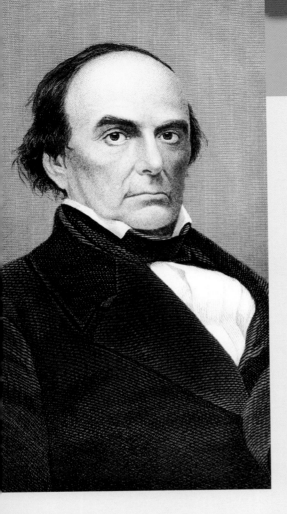

During the early 1800s, Daniel Webster was the most famous speaker in the United States. In his speeches, he argued for the country's need for a strong central government.

Webster was born in 1782 in Salisbury, New Hampshire. Today, this town is called Franklin. Webster served in the U.S. House of Representatives from 1813 to 1817. He later moved to Massachusetts. Voters there also elected him to the U.S. House of Representatives. He served from 1823 until 1827, when he became a U.S. senator from Massachusetts.

During his years in the Senate, Webster supported preserving the Union over the rights of the states. He supported the Compromise of 1850, which allowed slavery in some U.S. territories but not in others. Webster hoped this law would prevent a civil war. It did not.

Webster served in politics for most of his life. He ran for president in 1836 but was not elected. He served as U.S. secretary of state from 1841 to 1843 and again from 1850 until his death in 1852.

Recent Events

After World War II, New Hampshire built more highways. The highway system brought more tourists to the state.

In 1964, New Hampshire was the first state to start a lottery to fund its school system. In 2002, the state lottery provided $65 million for New Hampshire's public schools.

In January 1998, an ice storm hit the Northeast. Nine of New Hampshire's 10 counties declared a state of emergency. About 125,000 people in the state were left without power. The storm caused two deaths and about $130 million in damage to property and forests.

New Hampshire's capitol in Concord was built with granite from a nearby quarry.

Chapter 4

Government and Politics

New Hampshire's constitution was rewritten in 1783 and went into effect in 1784. The constitution has been amended many times since then. The constitution sets up the state's government, which includes the legislative, executive, and judicial branches.

Legislative Branch

The legislative branch is also known as the General Court of New Hampshire. It includes the house of representatives and the senate. With 24 senators and 400 representatives, New Hampshire has the largest legislature of any state. General Court members serve two-year terms.

Executive Branch

The governor is the leader of the executive branch. Unlike most states, New Hampshire does not have a lieutenant governor. A five-member council called the Executive Council advises the governor. The governor and members of the council are elected to two-year terms. They can serve an unlimited number of terms.

The governor manages all state agencies. The state agencies are responsible for New Hampshire's health, safety, education, and economic development.

Judicial Branch

New Hampshire's court system includes four courts. The four courts handle different types of cases. New Hampshire's 37 district courts hear cases about minor crimes and about property valued at $25,000 or less. Probate courts handle legal matters such as wills, name changes, and adoptions. The superior court hears cases involving more serious crimes. The superior court is the only court in New Hampshire where cases are decided by a jury.

New Hampshire's State Government

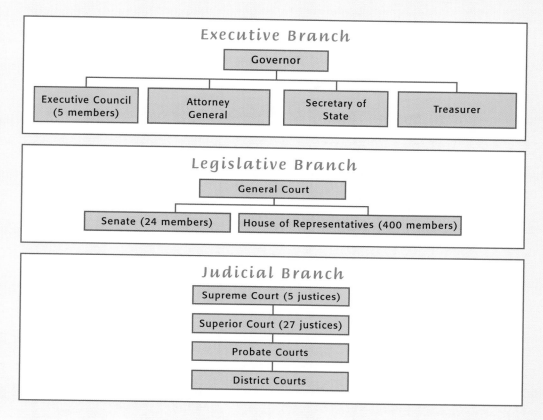

Executive Branch

Governor

| Executive Council (5 members) | Attorney General | Secretary of State | Treasurer |

Legislative Branch

General Court

| Senate (24 members) | House of Representatives (400 members) |

Judicial Branch

Supreme Court (5 justices)

Superior Court (27 justices)

Probate Courts

District Courts

The state supreme court is the highest court in New Hampshire. This court hears cases that have already been tried in district or superior courts. One chief justice and four associate justices serve on the court. The governor names the five supreme court justices. The Executive Council approves each justice's appointment. Justices serve until they retire.

Presidential Primaries

Since 1920, New Hampshire has held the first presidential primary election in the nation. At primaries, voters choose the party candidates who will run for office. The New Hampshire legislature established the presidential primary in 1913.

Every four years, presidential candidates travel to New Hampshire to campaign for the presidency. The primary election takes place in January. Several candidates from each political party campaign in New Hampshire.

Presidential candidate Al Gore campaigned in New Hampshire for the 2000 primary.

Politics in New Hampshire

New Hampshire holds more elections than most other states. It is one of only two states that elects its governor every two years. The other state is Vermont. Most states elect a governor every four years. On the second Tuesday in March, town meetings are held throughout the state. Citizens elect town leaders at these meetings.

The Republican Party became strong in New Hampshire before the Civil War. This party was against slavery. Most New Hampshirites also opposed slavery. The Democratic Party has become stronger in the state since the 1960s. But New Hampshire usually votes for the Republican Party candidate for president. The state had mostly Republican governors in the 1900s.

Union School
870 NW West Union Road
Hillsboro, Oregon 97124

Cross-country skiing is one of many outdoor activities tourists enjoy in New Hampshire.

Chapter 5

Economy and Resources

Since the 1800s, manufacturing and tourism have been the two most important industries in New Hampshire. The state's forests, stone, and other natural resources are made into many useful products. New Hampshire's cool summers provide an escape for people from Boston, New York City, and other crowded eastern cities. Tourists enjoy the state's scenery and outdoor activities.

Manufacturing

New Hampshire factories make a variety of products. These products include computer hardware and software, industrial equipment, and rubber and plastic products. Factories also produce furniture, flooring, cabinets, picture frames, and other wooden items. Some textile products are still made in the state. In 1957, the Swiss company Velcro moved its American operations to Manchester. Today, Velcro USA still has its headquarters there.

Since the Revolutionary War, New Hampshire factories have built ships and weapons for the U.S. military. The military needed fewer of these ships and weapons in the early 1990s. New Hampshire factories then began to produce more high-technology materials. By 2000, circuit

boards, computer software, and electronic parts were all growing industries in the state.

Tourism

Tourism is New Hampshire's second largest industry after manufacturing. Tourism brings more than $8.6 billion to the New Hampshire economy every year. More than 65,000 New Hampshirites work in the tourism industry.

Tourists enjoy New Hampshire during all four seasons. Skiing, snowmobiling, and sledding are popular winter

The Mount Washington Hotel in the White Mountains has 200 guest rooms and suites.

activities. In spring and summer, visitors golf, hike, camp, and fish. Fall brings thousands of visitors to see the colorful leaves.

Agriculture

In New Hampshire's early days, most of its people were farmers. Today, only 7 percent of its land is farmed. Major crops include hay and vegetables. Farmers also grow corn for animal feed. Other important crops include greenhouse

A logging truck hauls wood to this pulp plant in Berlin, New Hampshire. Wood pulp is used to make paper.

products, apples, Christmas trees, berries, maple syrup, and honey products.

New Hampshire farmers also raise livestock. The state's dairy farms produce more than 300 million gallons (1.1 billion liters) of milk each year. Farmers also raise chickens and other poultry for meat and eggs. Other farmers raise horses, cattle, sheep, and pigs. On small farms, people raise herds of llamas, alpacas, goats, and elk.

Logging

In the late 1800s, logging was a major business in New Hampshire. Almost all of the forests in the northern part of the state were cut down between 1867 and 1904.

The destruction of the forests led many New Hampshirites to fight to protect the forests. In 1901, eight citizens formed the Society for the Protection of New Hampshire Forests. This group bought and preserved forestland. They spoke to members of the U.S. Congress about saving the state's forests. In 1911, Congress passed the Weeks Act, which created White Mountain National Forest.

Granite is New Hampshire's largest mining industry. The state's largest granite quarries are near Concord.

Nearly 5 million acres (2 million hectares) of forests support the New Hampshire forest industry. Forestry brought almost $4 billion to the state's economy in 1998. About 16,000 New Hampshirites work in the forestry industry. This industry includes logging and sawmills.

Factories in the state make paper, furniture, and other wood products.

Wood energy is a growing part of the forestry industry. The first wood-powered energy plant in New Hampshire opened in 1982. By 2000, the state had five wood energy power plants. The fuel for these plants is made up of wood chip material that includes leaves, branches, and bark.

Mining

New Hampshire earned its nickname, the Granite State, from its rich deposits of granite. The state's largest granite quarries are near Concord. Granite is used in buildings. Granite from New Hampshire was used to build the Library of Congress in Washington, D.C.

People line up jack-o'-lanterns along Keene's Main Street for the Pumpkin Festival.

Chapter 6

People and Culture

Many events celebrate the seasons, the arts, and the way of life in New Hampshire. At these festivals, New Hampshirites and visitors enjoy the best of the state's music, crafts, and food.

The Pumpkin Festival in Keene is held the Saturday before Halloween. In 2000, the festival set a record for the most lighted jack-o'-lanterns in one place. Townspeople lined up 23,727 jack-o'-lanterns along the town's Main Street.

The League of New Hampshire Craftsmen's Fair has been held each August in Newbury since 1933. The nine-day fair features the work of more than 200 artists and craftspeople. Visitors can make their own crafts at hands-on demonstrations.

Population

Between 1990 and 2000, New Hampshire was the fastest growing Northeastern state. The population of New Hampshire grew 11 percent. The Northeast as a whole grew only 6 percent.

Of New Hampshire's regions, the Merrimack River Valley has the most people. The state's three largest cities are Manchester, Nashua, and Concord, the capital.

Ethnic Groups

In the 1800s and early 1900s, French-Canadian, English, Irish, and Finnish immigrants settled in New Hampshire. Many immigrants found work in the state's textile mills, logging camps, and granite quarries.

At one time, many American Indians lived in New Hampshire. Today, few American Indians remain in the state. New Hampshire has no Indian reservations.

New Hampshire's Ethnic Backgrounds

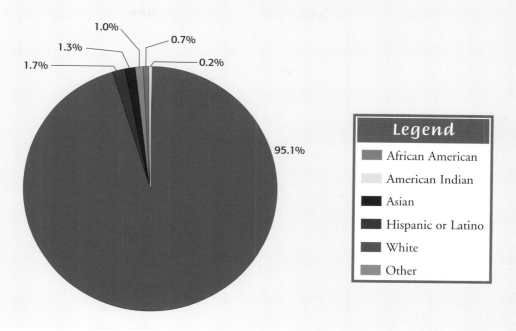

1.0%
1.3%
1.7%
0.7%
0.2%
95.1%

Legend
- African American
- American Indian
- Asian
- Hispanic or Latino
- White
- Other

Other ethnic groups in New Hampshire include Hispanics, African Americans, and Asian Americans. Together with American Indians, these groups make up less than 5 percent of the state's population.

Museums and Historic Sites

Manchester is known as a cultural center. Many art experts consider the Currier Museum of Art one of the best small art museums in the Northeast. Paintings by Pablo Picasso, Claude Monet, Georgia O'Keefe, and other famous artists hang in the museum. Manchester also is home to an opera company, several theaters, and the New Hampshire Philharmonic Orchestra.

Hanover is a historic New Hampshire town. In 1769, Reverend Eleazar Wheelock founded Dartmouth College in Hanover. Dartmouth is the ninth oldest college in the

country. Today, the college is known for offering one of the best educations in the country.

Concord became the state capital in 1808. Some of the city's buildings are more than 250 years old. The Reverend Timothy Walker House was built in 1734. It is believed to be the oldest two-story home between Massachusetts and Canada. The New Hampshire State Library is the oldest state library in the country. It was established in 1717.

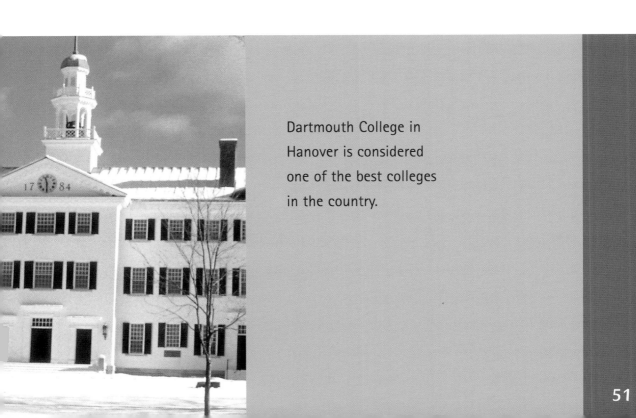

Dartmouth College in Hanover is considered one of the best colleges in the country.

Christa McAuliffe

In 1984, the National Aeronautics and Space Administration (NASA) decided to send an ordinary person into space. They wanted that person to be a teacher. The teacher would train with astronauts and fly on the space shuttle *Challenger*. NASA chose New Hampshire high school teacher Christa McAuliffe. McAuliffe planned to teach a lesson from space.

On January 28, 1986, the *Challenger* exploded 73 seconds after liftoff. The explosion killed everyone on board.

The Christa McAuliffe Planetarium opened in Concord in 1990. Almost 30,000 children visit the planetarium each year to learn about space science and astronomy.

Famous New Hampshirites

New Hampshire has produced many well-known writers. John Irving was born in Exeter. His books include *The Hotel New Hampshire, The Cider House Rules,* and *A Prayer for Owen Meany*. Poet Robert Frost was born in California, but

he lived in and wrote about New Hampshire for many years. He received four Pulitzer Prizes for his poetry. J. D. Salinger was born in New York City but has lived in New Hampshire since the 1950s. He wrote the popular book *The Catcher in the Rye.*

An Independent State

The independent spirit of New Hampshire's people is shown in the state's motto, "Live Free or Die." Throughout this small state's history, its people have found ways to make life better in their state. They have made good use of the state's natural resources. They replaced declining industries with new ones. They passed laws that improved living and working conditions. New Hampshirites look forward to a strong economy and good living conditions in the future.

Recipe: Maple Syrup Muffins

Maple syrup is one of New Hampshire's major food products. Maple syrup provides the flavoring for these moist, rich muffins.

Ingredients

½ cup (120 mL) shortening
2 eggs
½ cup (120 mL) maple syrup
½ cup (120 mL) milk
2 cups (480 mL) flour
4 teaspoons (20 mL) baking powder
½ teaspoon (2.5 mL) salt

Equipment

2 muffin pans
muffin cup liners
2 medium bowls
electric mixer
fork
oven mitts

What You Do

1. Preheat oven to 350°F (180°C).

2. Put muffin cup liners in the muffin pan cups.

3. In medium bowl, mix shortening and eggs with electric mixer until well blended.

4. Add syrup and milk to egg mixture. Mix well with electric mixer.

5. In second medium bowl, mix flour, baking powder, and salt with fork.

6. Add flour mixture to egg mixture. Mix well.

7. Fill each muffin cup liner about two-thirds full with batter.

8. Bake 20 to 25 minutes or until muffins are lightly browned.

9. With oven mitts, remove muffin pans from oven.

10. After the muffins are cool, remove them from the pans.

Makes 16 servings

New Hampshire's Flag and Seal

New Hampshire's Flag

New Hampshire adopted its state flag in 1909. The flag was changed slightly in 1931 when the legislature adopted an official state seal. The flag is dark blue. The state seal is in the center. Laurel leaves and nine stars surround the seal. The stars represent New Hampshire's position as the ninth state.

New Hampshire's State Seal

The New Hampshire state seal was first created in 1775. Many changes were made over the years. The legislature created a permanent seal in 1931. The words "Seal of the State of New Hampshire, 1776" wrap around the circle. The warship *Raleigh* is in the center of the seal. Built in 1776, the *Raleigh* was one of the first Navy warships. A wreath of laurel leaves surrounds the *Raleigh*. A granite boulder near the ship stands for the state's rocky land.

Almanac

General Facts

Nickname: Granite State

Population: 1,235,786
(U.S. Census, 2000)
Population rank: 41st

Capital: Concord

Largest communities:
Manchester, Nashua,
Concord, Derry, Rochester

Agriculture

Agricultural products:
Dairy products,
greenhouse products,
maple syrup, hay, feed
corn, apples, vegetables

Climate

**Average summer
temperature:**
65 degrees Fahrenheit
(18 degrees Celsius)

**Average winter
temperature:**
20 degrees Fahrenheit
(minus 7 degrees Celsius)

**Average annual
precipitation:** 42 inches
(107 centimeters)

Geography

Area: 9,351 square miles
(24,219 square kilometers)
Size rank: 44th

Highest point: Mount
Washington, 6,288 feet
(1,917 meters) above
sea level

Lowest point: Atlantic coast,
sea level

Purple lilac

Ladybugs

Economy

Natural resources: Granite and other types of stone, trees

Types of industry: Tourism, logging, machinery, electrical and computer equipment, textiles, rubber and plastic products

Amphibian: Red-spotted newt

Animal: White-tailed deer

Bird: Purple finch

Flower: Purple lilac

Gem: Smoky quartz

Symbols

Insect: Ladybug

Rock: Granite

Song: "Old New Hampshire," by Dr. John F. Holmes and Maurice Hoffmann

Tree: White birch

Symbols

First governor: John Langdon, 1788–1789, 1805–1809, 1810–1812

Statehood: June 21, 1788 (9th state)

U.S. Representatives: 2

U.S. Senators: 2

U.S. electoral votes: 4

Counties: 10

Government

Timeline

State History

1600
About 5,000 members of the Abenaki and Pennacook Confederacies are living in present-day New Hampshire when French and British explorers arrive.

1641
The first New Hampshire colonies unite under Massachusetts' rule.

1679
King Charles II divides New Hampshire and Massachusetts into separate colonies.

1788
New Hampshire becomes the ninth state on June 21.

1809
The first textile mill is built near Manchester.

U.S. History

1620
Pilgrims establish a colony in the New World.

1763
Great Britain wins the French and Indian War.

1775–1783
American colonists fight for independence from Great Britain in the Revolutionary War.

1861–1865
The Union and the Confederacy fight the Civil War.

Greetings From NEW HAMPSHIRE
USA 34
2002

1913
New Hampshire holds its first presidential primary.

1964
New Hampshire becomes the first state to hold a lottery to benefit its school system.

1998
A severe ice storm kills two people and causes much property damage.

1986
New Hampshire teacher Christa McAuliffe is killed when the space shuttle *Challenger* explodes.

1929–1939
Many Americans lose jobs during the Great Depression.

1964
U.S. Congress passes the Civil Rights Act, which makes any form of discrimination illegal.

1914–1918
World War I is fought; the United States enters the war in 1917.

1939–1945
World War II is fought; the United States enters the war in 1941.

2001
On September 11, terrorists attack the World Trade Center and the Pentagon.

Words to Know

colony (KOL-uh-nee)—land governed by another country; a group of people who leave their own country to settle in a colony are called colonists.

earthquake (URTH-kwayk)—a sudden, violent shaking of the ground; a shifting of Earth's crust causes this shaking.

glacier (GLAY-shur)—a large mass of slowly moving ice

granite (GRAN-it)—a hard, gray rock often used for buildings and gravestones

immigrant (IM-uh-gruhnt)—a person who comes to another country to live permanently

planetarium (plan-uh-TAIR-ee-uhm)—a building where visitors see images of the movements of the Sun, Moon, planets, and stars projected on a curved ceiling

primary election (PRYE-mair-ee e-LEHK-shuhn)—an election in which voters choose the party candidates who will run for office

quarry (KWOR-ee)—a place where people dig or cut stone from the ground

textile (TEK-stile)—thread, yarn, or cloth that has been woven or knitted

tide (TIDE)—the constant change in sea level that is caused by the pull of the Moon and the Sun on Earth

To Learn More

Harvey, Bonnie C. *Daniel Webster: Liberty and Union, Now and Forever.* Historical American Biographies. Berkeley Heights, N.J.: Enslow Publishers, 2001.

Ingram, Scott. *The Battle of Bunker Hill.* Revolutionary War Battles. San Diego: Blackbirch Press, 2004.

Shannon, Terry Miller. *New Hampshire.* From Sea to Shining Sea. New York: Children's Press, 2002.

Stein, R. Conrad. *New Hampshire.* America the Beautiful. New York: Children's Press, 2000.

Internet Sites

Do you want to find out more about New Hampshire?
Let FactHound, our fact-finding hound dog, do the research for you.

Here's how:
1) Visit ***http://www.facthound.com***
2) Type in the **Book ID** number: **0736821872**
3) Click on **FETCH IT**.

FactHound will fetch Internet sites picked by our editors just for you!

Places to Write and Visit

Christa McAuliffe Planetarium
2 Institute Drive
Concord, NH 03301

Museum of New Hampshire History
The Hamel Center
6 Eagle Square
Concord, NH 03301-4923

New Hampshire Division of Travel and Tourism Development
172 Pembroke Road
P.O. Box 1856
Concord, NH 03302-1856

Portsmouth Naval Shipyard Museum and Visitor Center
Building 31
Portsmouth Naval Shipyard
Portsmouth, NH 03804-5000

Reverend Timothy Walker House
276 North Main Street
Concord, NH 03302

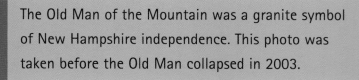

The Old Man of the Mountain was a granite symbol of New Hampshire independence. This photo was taken before the Old Man collapsed in 2003.